Opera Plots Made Easy

Pocket Dictionary of Opera Plots

G000168048

DEAVER

Deaver Corporation
New York

In memory of M.L.D.

Revised Edition: 1991

Copyright 1984, 1988, & 1991
by Robert Deaver

Printed in the United States of America
by DEAVER CORPORATION, NEW YORK CITY

ISBN 0-932665-00-4

INTRODUCTION

This book is for the opera goer, student, and expert. It tells "at a glance" what each opera is about.

Opera Plots Made Easy, is written in clear, modern language...and has large, readable print. Its plots make sense and can be remembered.

Use this book to decide which operas to attend...which opera series to subscribe to...and as a basis for conversation.

This book makes opera more interesting and enjoyable. Take it with you to the opera. It fits easily in pocket or purse...and quickly tells what is going on.

CONTENTS

ABDUCTION FROM THE SERAGLIO

Mozart

Comic opera about captives trying to escape a Turkish harem.

Constanza, a lady; Blonda, her maid; and Pedrillio, the maid's boyfriend, have been captured and sold into slavery. Belmonte comes to free them.

Act 1 In front of Pasha's palace, Belmonte asks the haremkeeper to free Constanza...but is refused. Pedrillio introduces Belmonte to Pasha as a "visiting architect."

Act 2 Blonda warns Osmin, the haremkeeper, to leave her alone. Pedrillio gets the haremkeeper drunk, so the captives can escape.

Act 3 They are caught leaving. The Pasha forgives...and lets them go.

AIDA

Verdi

Love story between Ethiopian slave girl, Aida, and captain of the Egyptian guard, Radames.

Act 1 Radames, hopes to become general of the Egyptian army and marry Aida. But, Egyptian king's daughter, Amneris, also loves him.

Act 2 Radames and the Egyptian army return in triumph from war... having captured Aida's father, the Ethiopian king.

Act 3 Aida persuades Radames to betray the Egyptian army. Radames then surrenders to the Egyptian priests.

Act 4 The priests bury prisoner Radames alive in a tomb, where Aida has hidden. Princess Amneris weeps at the entrance to the tomb.

BALLAD OF BABY DOE

Moore

A true love story between the once-wealthy Colorado silver mine owner, Horace Tabor...and his second wife, Baby Doe.

Act 1 Horace Tabor, mayor of Leadville, Colorado leaves the opera house bored...and is called back in by his domineering first wife, Augusta. In the meantime, the pretty Baby Doe arrives in town, and Horace gives her directions to the hotel. Horace divorces Augusta, marries Baby Doe, and is appointed U.S. Senator.

Act 2 The "ladies" in town shun Horace's new wife, Baby Doe. Horace risks too much on the future of silver mining...trying to keep his "Matchless Mine"...and eventually he goes broke.

BARBER OF SEVILLE

Rossini

Comic opera about a Count and his girlfriend trying to get married ...assisted by a busybody "barber."

Act 1 Count Almaviva serenades Rosina...but Rosina's guardian, Dr. Bartolo, won't let her see the Count. Her guardian, instead, wants to marry Rosina.

The barber plots with the Count ...who disguises himself as a drunk soldier, newly assigned to live in Bartolo's house. Disruption ensues, and the police arrive.

Act 2 The Count comes to Bartolo's house disguised as a "professor"...to substitute for Rosina's supposedly-sick music teacher. The Count, with the barber's help, manages to marry Rosina.

LA BOHEME

Puccini

Opera with lush, rich music. Paris in the early-1800's...poor, struggling artists...and LOVE!

Act 1 Rodolfo, a poet; Marcello, a painter; Colline, a philosopher; and Schaunard, a musician, outwit landlord come to collect rent. Rodolfo meets Mimi, a seamstress who has come to light her candle.

Act 2 At outdoor cafe, Marcello sees his old girlfriend, Musetta... who sends her escort on a false errand.

Act 3 Outside inn at edge of Paris Rodolfo and Mimi decide to separate.

Act 4 Mimi is dying.   Musetta sells her earrings to buy medicine ...but to no avail!

CARMEN

Bizet

Love story between a sensuous, bold, Gypsy girl, Carmen, and the soldier, Don Jose.

Act 1 In Spain outside a cigarette factory, Don Jose arrests Carmen for causing a disturbance. She gives him seductive promises...and he lets her escape...for which he is arrested.

Act 2 At an inn, Carmen welcomes Don Jose after his release from jail. Don Jose joins a band of smugglers.

Act 3 In the mountains, Micaela, Don Jose's old girlfriend, comes looking for him. She tells Don Jose his Mother is dying, and he leaves Carmen to go to his Mother.

Act 4 Carmen has become the lover of a bullfighter. Jealous, Don Jose kills Carmen.

CAVALLERIA RUSTICANA
(Rustic Chivalry)

Mascagni

An opera of strong passions... jealousy, love, and tragic death.

Act 1 Easter Sunday in the main square of a Sicilian village. The girl, Santuzza, is worried that her fiance, Turiddu, is having an affair with Lola, wife of Alfio.

Outside the Church, Santuzza tells her problem to Mamma Lucia, mother of Turiddu, but receives no help.

Santuzza appeals to Turiddu, her fiance, but he pushes her to the ground. Then, Santuzza tells Alfio, Lola's husband.

After the Church service, Alfio challenges Turiddu to a duel and kills him!

11

CENERENTOLA
(Cinderella)

Rossini

A slightly different version of "Cinderella" in opera form.

Act 1 The Prince switches clothes with his valet...because he wants to be loved for himself...and meets Cinderella at her stepfather's home.

The Prince's philosopher, Alidoro, arranges for Cinderella to come to the ball.

Act 2 At the ball Cinderella, wearing a mask, gives the Prince, disguised as his valet, one of a set of bracelets.

The Prince, now dressed as himself, comes to Cinderella's home ...and finds she is wearing the matching bracelet. Love and happiness!

THE CONSUL

Menotti

The hopeless paperwork and frustration faced by people trying to leave a "police state" country.

Act 1 John Sorel, wounded by the secret police, comes home. The police arrive; he escapes through a window; and his wife, Magda, is questioned. Magda goes to a consulate and hopelessly fills out forms to leave the country.

Act 2 A window is broken in Magda's home; the repairman brings news of John. More waiting in the consulate for Magda.

Act 3 John hurries into the consulate looking for Magda...and is captured by the police. At home, Magda puts her head in the oven and dies from the gas.

COSI FAN TUTTE
(School for Lovers)

Mozart

Comic opera about the "loyalty" of lovers.

Act 1 At a cafe, two young soldiers, Ferrando and Guglielmo, argue with an old man, Don Alfonso, about the loyalty of their girlfriends. He bets their girlfriends will be unfaithful.

The men pretend to go away to war...then return disguised...and try to date each other's previous girlfriend.

Act 2 The girls, sisters named Fiordiligi and Dorabella, fall for the deception...helped along by their maid, Despina.

All is revealed and forgiven.

DAUGHTER OF THE REGIMENT
(Fille du Regiment)

Donizetti

Comic opera about a girl, Marie, raised by a French army regiment. Marie finds love, and marriage, with a brave peasant, Tonio, who joins the regiment.

Act 1 The regiment wins a battle. Marie, dressed as a little drummer girl sings in celebration.

A strange young man, Tonio, is discovered. Marie explains how Tonio saved her life. Tonio joins the regiment to be with Marie.

A wealthy lady, Marquise de Birkenfeld, finds Marie is her long-lost-niece...and takes her away.

Act 2 Marie is a misfit at the lady's home. When her regiment marches by...Marie joins it, and her boyfriend Tonio, with a celebration!

DON CARLOS

Verdi

A father-wife-son love triangle.

Act 1 King Philip married his son Carlos' promised bride, Elizabeth. Rodrigo advises Carlos go to Flanders and forget Elizabeth.

Act 2 Carlos is invited to a mysterious rendezvous. The veiled lady is Princess Eboli...instead of his love, Elizabeth. Carlos asks in vain for his father to send him to Flanders.

Act 3 King Philip senses Queen Elizabeth never loved him...and is jealous of his son, Carlos. Carlos is put in prison.

Act 4 Elizabeth and Carlos meet in a convent...and are discovered. Carlos' grandfather's ghost drags Carlos to safety into a tomb!

DON GIOVANNI
(Don Juan)

Mozart

Don (Juan's) Giovanni's loves and conquests...in a comic opera.

Act 1 Assisted by Leporello, his servant, the Don courts Anna...kills her father in a fight...and escapes her boyfriend, Don Ottavio.

The Don encounters an old love, Elvira, and manages to escape.

Then he meets Zerlina, whose boyfriend, Masetto, is suspicious.

Act 2 The Don changes clothes with his servant, Leporello, Then, much confusion as to who is whom.

As a joke, the Don invites a statue of Anna's dead father to dinner. When the statue actually comes, the Don's palace disappears in flames as punishment for his sins.

DON PASQUALE

Donizetti

Comedy about the folly of an old man trying to marry a young girl.

Act 1 An old, wealthy bachelor, Don Pasquale, asks his friend, Malatesta, to find him a young wife. Unfortunately, Pasquale's marriage will disinherit his nephew, Ernesto.

Malatesta plans to pass off Ernesto's girlfriend, Norina, as a possible wife for Pasquale.

Act 2 A fake marriage is arranged, and the mild Norina pretends to become a selfish spendthrift.

Act 3 Pasquale feels having another woman in his house will drive his bride away. Thus, he permits his nephew, Ernesto, to marry. Surprise! Ernesto's bride is the same Norina; Pasquale is glad his painful marriage was a fake.

ELIXIR OF LOVE
(Elisir d'amore)

Donizetti

Comic opera about a love potion (wine) sold by a quack, Dr. Dulcamara.

Act 1 Adina, a wealthy girl, is loved by both Nemorino, a shy peasant, and by Sergeant Belcore.

Nemorino spends all his money for a love potion that will, he thinks, cause Adina to love him in 24-hours. Unfortunately, Adina promises to marry Sergeant Belcore that very night.

Act 2 Nemorino enlists in the army...and spends his enlistment bonus on an elixir supposed to work in 1/2 hour (more wine). Reckless and confident from the wine, Nemorino attracts Adina...who buys back his enlistment.

ERNANI

Verdi

Ernani, Don Silva, and King Carlos all want to marry Elvira.

Act 1 Ernani, a bandit of noble birth, goes to rescue Elvira from Silva--her guardian, who wants to marry her.

Act 2 At Silva's castle, Ernani interrupts the wedding between Elvira and Silva. King Carlos comes also...and takes away Elvira. Ernani and Silva decide to unite against the King...to rescue Elvira.

Act 3 The King captures Ernani and Silva at a cathedral burial vault. News comes that the King is now an Emperor...and he pardons Ernani and Silva.

Act 4 Ernani has married Elvira. Ernani commits suicide to fulfill a promise to Silva.

EUGENE ONEGIN

Tchaikovsky

Eugene Onegin scorns Tatiana's love. Later, when Onegin falls in love with Tatiana, she rejects him.

Act 1 Onegin and his friend, Lensky, visit Tatiana and her sister, Olga. Tatiana writes a love letter to Onegin.

Onegin tells Tatiana he isn't interested in marrying her.

Act 2 At a party, Onegin dances repeatedly with Lensky's fiancee, Olga. Jealous, Lensky challenges him to a duel...and is killed.

Act 3 Tatiana has married Prince Gremin. When Onegin sees Tatiana at a dance, he realizes he loves her. He writes to her...and when they meet privately, she rejects his love.

FALSTAFF

Verdi

Comic opera about an old Knight, Falstaff, trying to seduce married women, Mistress Ford and Mistress Page, to obtain money from them.

Act 1 Falstaff and his drinking buddies, Bardolph and Pistol, need money to pay the innkeeper.

Falstaff sends love letters to Mistress Ford and Mistress Page... who decide to play a trick on him.

Act 2 At Mistress Ford's house, Falstaff hides when her husband returns. Then, the laundry basket Falstaff is hiding in is thrown out a window...into the river!

Act 3 Falstaff is invited to a midnight rendezvous with Mistress Ford in a park...but he is tricked again, and frightened by people in ghostly disguises.

FAUST

Gounod

An old philosopher, Faust, sells his soul to Mephistopheles, the devil...to be young again.

Act 1 Faust strikes a bargain with Mephistopheles. On earth, Faust is the master...later he will serve Mephistopheles. Faust and Mephistopheles go off together seeking adventure.

Act 2 Faust romances Marguerite ...and has Mephistopheles prepare a gift of jewels for her.

Act 3 In Church, Marguerite prays that her sins be pardoned. Her brother, Valentine, returns from war and dies fighting Faust.

Act 4 Marguerite is in prison for killing her child. She prays to God...and is saved!

FIDELIO

Beethoven

A woman, Leonora, disguises herself as a man (becoming Fidelio) ...in order to rescue her imprisoned husband, Florestan.

Act 1 Leonora disguises herself as "Fidelio," and takes a job as assistant to Rocco--the senior jailer. Unfortunately, Rocco's daughter, Marcellina, falls in love with "Fidelio."

Pizarro, head of the prison, orders a grave dug for his secret prisoner, Florestan.

Act 2 Pizarro comes to kill Florestan...and Fidelio (Leonora) points her gun at Pizarro. The Prime Minister, Don Fernando, arrives; recognizes Leonora and Florestan as his friends; and has Pizarro imprisoned, instead.

FLEDERMAUS
(The Bat)

Johann Strauss

Comic operetta with lively music.

Act 1 Alfred, a former boyfriend, serenades Rosalinda--Eisenstein's wife. Rosalinda's maid, Adele, wants the night off...to attend a party. Eisenstein must report to jail that night...for a minor offense. Instead, he decides to go to a party ...and report to jail in the morning.

Act 2 The party is a masked ball thrown by Prince Orlofsky... where Eisenstein doesn't recognize his own masked wife...who flirts with him and takes his watch.

Act 3 In the morning Eisenstein reports to jail...and finds Alfredo (found in Eisenstein's home and mistaken for Eisenstein) had been captured and taken to jail instead.

FLYING DUTCHMAN

Wagner

The Flying Dutchman is captain of a ship doomed to travel forever, or until he finds a faithful woman.

Act 1 The Dutchman's strange ship anchors next to Captain Daland's ship. Finding that Daland has a daughter, the Dutchman proposes to marry her.

Act 2 Captain Dalland's daughter, Senta, tells how she is in love with the legendary Flying Dutchman.

Act 3 Eric, an old boyfriend, pleads with Senta to give up her love for the Flying Dutchman. Hearing this, the Dutchman prepares to sail away. Senta jumps off a cliff into the ocean...to demonstrate her "faithfulness until death." This releases the Dutchman from his fate.

FORZA DEL DESTINO
(Force of Destiny)

Verdi

A love between Leonora and Alvaro that is "doomed" by fate.

Act 1 Leonora and Alvaro are about to elope when interrupted by her father. Alvaro accidentally kills her father.

Act 2 Leonora's brother, Carlo, swears to kill Leonora and Alvaro. Leonora, disguised as a man, avoids discovery by her brother. Leonora becomes a recluse living in a cave.

Act 3 Alvaro saves Carlo's life, neither one recognizing the other. Carlo later learns Alvaro's identity.

Act 4 Near Leonora's cave, Carlo duels with Alvaro, and Carlo is wounded. When Leonora tries to help her dying brother, he stabs her.

FREISCHUTZ
(The Free-Shooter)

Weber

A shooting contest is used to determine who will marry the head forest ranger, Kuno's daughter, Agathe.

Act 1 The day before the big contest, Max is disappointed at losing a shooting contest. Caspar, a rival, tells him "magic," free shots that won't miss are available from Zamiel, the devil.

Act 2 Caspar summons the devil, and Max and Caspar receive magic bullets.

Act 3 Agathe has a bad dream about the contest. Max's last shot, directed by the devil, kills Caspar. A wise hermit advises Prince Ottokar to put Max on a year's probation... and then let Max marry Agathe. Joy and celebration!

GIANNI SCHICCHI

Puccini

Comic opera about how the greedy relatives of a wealthy man are out-smarted!

Act 1 Buoso Donati has just died, and his will leaves everything to a monastery...and nothing to his relatives.

Rinuccio, Donati's nephew, wants to marry Lauretta...the daughter of a shrewd peasant, Gianni Schicchi. Lauretta asks her father to help... so they will have some money.

Donati's body is removed...and Schicchi takes Donati's place in bed. A lawyer is brought in, and Schicchi dictates the old man's "new" will, leaving everything to... Schicchi! The relatives are angry ...but can do nothing, since they aided the deception.

GIOCONDA
(The Ballad Singer)

Ponchielli

The misfortunes of Gioconda, a girl who is a street singer in 17th-century Venice.

Act 1 Barnaba, an Inquisition spy, accuses Gioconda's blind mother, Cieca, of being a witch. Enzo saves them from the crowd.

Act 2 Laura, Duke Alvise's wife, and Enzo meet on Enzo's ship. Gioconda comes to warn them that Alvise is approaching.

Act 3 Alvise tells his wife, Laura, she must poison herself...because of her unfaithfulness. Gioconda gives her a harmless, sleep-inducing drug. Gioconda promises herself to the evil Barnaba to save Enzo.

Act 4 Gioconda stabs herself to prevent Barnaba from having her.

GIRL OF THE GOLDEN WEST
(Fanciulla del West)

Puccini

Love story set in the mid-1850's American West. Minni, a saloon owner falls in love with Ramerrez (alias Dick Johnson) a bandit she persuades to quit his life of crime.

Act 1 At Minnie's barroom Rance, the sheriff, wants to marry Minnie. A stranger, "Dick Johnson," comes in...and Minnie is attracted to him.

Act 2 Because of a snowstorm, Minnie invites Dick Johnson (Ramerrez) to stay at her cabin. Rance, the sheriff, wounds Johnson ...but Minnie saves Johnson by playing a game of poker with Rance.

Act 3 Johnson (Ramerrez) is captured by the miners, but Minnie persuades them to set him free.

GOTTERDAMMERUNG
(Twilight of the Gods)

Wagner

Events leading to the end of the gods and their castle, Valhalla.

Prologue The gods wait at Valhalla for the end. Siegfried, a great hero, emerges from a cave with Brunnhilde...whom he weds by giving his magic ring. Siegfried goes off to do great deeds.

Act 1 Hagen and Gunther plot to get the magic ring. They give Siegfried a memory-erasing drink and send him for Brunnhilde.

Act 2 Siegfried returns with Brunnhilde and the magic ring.

Act 3 Hagen kills Siegfried. Brunnhilde joins Siegfried on a burning funeral pyre. Rhinemaidens get the golden ring. Fire spreads and destroys the gods at Valhalla.

HANSEL AND GRETEL

Humperdinck

The classic fairy tale.

Act 1 A poor broommaker, Peter, and his wife, Gertrude, live in a cottage in Germany. Their children, Hansel and Gretel, are hungry, and go into the forest for strawberries.

Act 2 At dusk the children fall asleep in each other's arms...angels guard them through the night.

Act 3 When dawn comes, they see a cottage decorated with child-sized gingerbread figures. A witch puts Hansel in a cage. Gretel is forced to work for the witch.

Gretel pushes the witch into the oven. There is an explosion that turns the gingerbread figures back into children. Peter and Gertrude arrive for a happy reunion with Hansel and Gretel.

LAKME

Delibes

Love story, in colonial India, between British Army Officer, Gerald, and Hindu Priest's daughter, Lakme.

Act 1 British Army Officers, Gerald and Frederick, escort their friends, Ellen and Rose, into a sacred Hindu garden. Gerald stays on to draw a picture of Lakme's jewelry. When Lakme and Gerald see each other, they fall in love.

Act 2 Nilakantha, Lakme's father, searches for the Englishman who violated the sacred garden. Nilakantha has Lakme sing in the city bazaar to draw the intruder forth. He stabs Gerald.

Act 3 In a cave, Lakme nurses Gerald back to health. When she fears he will return to his army, Lakme poisons herself.

LOHENGRIN

Wagner

Elsa's honor is defended in combat by the knight, Lohengrin... whom she marries...then loses.

Act 1 Telramund accuses Elsa of killing her young brother, Godfrey. Elsa's innocence is determined in a "trial by combat." Her champion arrives in a boat pulled by a swan. He agrees to defend her if she will marry him...and never ask his name or where he is from.

Act 2 Elsa's wedding is interrupted by Ortrud, Telramund's wife, and later by Telramund...who want to know the knight's name.

Act 3 Elsa asks his name. He answers, Lohengrin, of Monsalvat. Lohengrin leaves, and a swan is changed into Elsa's missing brother.

LOUISE

Charpentier

Love story, in early-1900's Paris, between working-class girl, Louise, and her poet-boyfriend, Julien.

Act 1 Louise and Julien stand on each side of a window talking and courting. Louise's poor parents don't want her to marry a poet.

Act 2 Julien and his friends go to the dressmaker's shop where Louise works and "serenade" her.

Act 3 The young lovers have moved to a house of their own; they are happy with their friends and life there. Louise's mother comes, saying Louise's father is sick...and wanting Louise to come home.

Act 4 Louise fights with her parents and returns to her lover. Her parents are shocked at losing Louise.

LUCIA DI LAMMERMOOR
Donizetti

Lucia's brother, Enrico, forces her into a "marriage of convenience" to Arturo--whom she does not love. This drives Lucia crazy, and she kills her husband.

Act 1 Enrico needs money and wants his sister, Lucia, to marry the wealthy Arturo. Instead, Lucia loves Edgardo, who saved her life.

Act 2 Lucia's brother, Enrico, has intercepted all the letters from her boyfriend, Edgardo. Then, he forges a false letter saying Edgardo has married someone else! Dazed and broken by this letter, Lucia does her brother's bidding and marries Arturo.

Act 3 Driven crazy, Lucia kills Arturo. Hearing the sad events, Edgardo, her boyfriend, commits suicide.

MADAM BUTTERFLY

Puccini

A 15-year-old Japanese girl's hopeless marriage to an American sailor. Lush, beautiful music.

Act 1 Marriage broker, Goro, arranges a union between Lieutenant Pinkerton and Madam Butterfly (Cio-Cio-San). Sharpless, the American Consul, warns Pinkerton he is not taking the marriage seriously. Butterfly's family rejects her for marrying a foreigner.

Act 2 Pinkerton has been gone for three years. Yamadori, a Japanese man, wants to marry Butterfly, but she refuses...saying she is already married.

Act 3 Pinkerton and his American wife, Kate, arrive. Butterfly kills herself!

MAGIC FLUTE

Mozart

Prince Tamino uses a magic flute to rescue Princess Pamina.

Act 1 Tamino is saved from a snake by three ladies who attend Queen of the Night. A birdcatcher, Papageno, takes credit for killing the snake...and is punished by the ladies for lying.

Queen of the Night sends Tamino and Papageno to rescue her daughter, Pamina, from Sarastro. She gives Tamino a magic flute, and Papageno magic bells, to help them.

Act 2 Tamino and Papageno face a series of tests from Sarastro. Tamino ends up with Pamina...and Papageno with his new girlfriend, Papagena. Thunder and lightning ...and the forces of evil disappear.

MANON

Massenet

A pure, sheltered girl, Manon, yields to her craving for a life of luxury, excitement, and love.

Act 1 Traveling to a convent, Manon stops at an inn. There she falls in love with des Grieux...and they go off to Paris together.

Act 2 Manon and des Grieux are living together in Paris. Des Grieux is kidnapped. Manon takes up with De Bretigny, who gives her beautiful, expensive things.

Act 3 Des Grieux is studying to become a priest. Manon goes to him and persuades him to leave.

Act 4 Manon and des Grieux are arrested.

Act 5 Manon, being deported to Louisiana, dies in des Grieux' arms.

MANON LESCAUT

Puccini

A young girl headed for a convent chooses, instead, a life of pleasure...with unfortunate results.

Act 1 Manon's carriage stops at an inn, where she meets her brother, Lescaut. She falls in love with Des Grieux...and they run off to Paris together.

Act 2 Manon leaves Des Grieux for the wealthy Geronte. Des Grieux arrives and persuades Manon to leave with him...but Geronte has Manon arrested.

Act 3 Lescaut and Des Grieux try to free Manon...but fail. Manon is being deported to Louisiana, and Des Grieux joins her on the ship.

Act 4 In Louisiana, Manon is ill ...and dies in Des Grieux' arms.

MARRIAGE OF FIGARO

Mozart

Comic opera with lively music.

Acts 1 & 2 Count Almaviva's valet, Figaro, wants to marry Susanna, the household's maid. But, Marcellina, Dr. Bartolo's old housekeeper wants Figaro to marry her. Count Almaviva also has designs on Susanna. And, Almaviva's young page, Cherubino, is girl-crazy. As a result, there is much hiding behind, and under, things and jumping out of windows.

Act 3 Dr. Bartolo and his housekeeper, Marcellina, are found to be Figaro's father and mother...and they decide to get married at the same time as Figaro and Susanna.

Act 4 At night in the garden, Count Almaviva thinks he is meeting Susanna; instead it is his wife!

MARTHA

Flotow

A comedy where Lady Harriet and her lady-in-waiting, Nancy, disguise themselves as farm maids...with interesting results.

Act 1 Lady Harriet and Nancy disguise themselves as "Martha" and "Julia"...and hire themselves out as maids to Lionel and Plunkett.

Act 2 "Martha" and "Julia" know nothing of the work required on a farm! With the aid of Sir Tristam, the girls escape from the farm.

Act 3 Lionel and Plunkett see their supposed "maids" ride by as ladies-in-waiting to Queen Anne. Lionel is arrested.

Act 4 Lionel is found to be the Earl of Derby! Lady Harriet persuades him to marry her.

MASKED BALL
(Ballo in maschera)

Verdi

King Riccardo is killed at a masked ball by his trusted aide, Renato.

Act 1 Riccardo is attracted to Amelia, his aide Renato's wife.

Riccardo visits Ulrica, the fortuneteller...and disregards her warning that the next person to shake his hand will kill him...this turns out to be Renato.

Act 2 Renato comes upon Amelia, his wife, with Riccardo. Conspirators, Samuele and Tommaso, draw lots with Renato to decide who will kill Riccardo.

Act 3 Oscar, a page, is persuaded to reveal Riccardo's disguise at the masked ball...and Renato kills Riccardo.

MEFISTOFELE

Boito

The Devil, Mefistofele, bets with God he can tempt Faust into sin... and thus have his soul.

Act 1 The old philosopher, Faust, with his student, Wagner, walks through the crowd on Easter Sunday. Later the devil offers to serve Faust on Earth, if Faust will serve him in Hell. Faust agrees.

Act 2 Faust is now a young man and courts Margherite. Faust has a vision of Margherite in chains.

Act 3 Margherite is in prison for poisoning her mother and drowning her child. She prays and receives salvation.

Act 4 Faust courts Helen of Troy.

Epilogue Again old, Faust prays for salvation...and escapes Hell.

MEISTERSINGER
(The Mastersingers)

Wagner

Walther enters, and wins, a singing contest...where the prize is
marriage to the beautiful Eva.

Act 1 Walther admires Eva and
wants to enter the singing contest
...so he can marry her. Walther
auditions for the mastersingers
guild...but is rejected.

Act 2 Walther and Eva try to
elope during some confusion and
arguing in the street in front of
her house...but are stopped from
doing so by Hans Sachs--a cobbler,
who is also a member of the singing
guild.

Act 3 Walther sings in, and wins,
the contest. He wins the hand of
Eva...and will inherit her father's
wealth.

NORMA

Bellini

A love story in Gaul between a noble Druid priestess, Norma, and Roman Proconsul, Pollione.

Act 1 High priest, Oroveso, gathers the Druids and tells them his daughter, the high priestess Norma, will signal them when to rise up against the Roman occupiers.

Act 2 Norma has violated her oath of chastity and borne two of Roman Proconsul Pollione's children. Pollione now loves another Druid priestess, Adalgisa.

Act 3 Norma intends to kill her children...but is unable to. She summons her rival, Adalgisa, and they become reconciled.

Act 4 Norma honorably decides to be burned to death, and Pollione chooses to die with her.

OTELLO

Verdi

Tragedy where Otello wrongfully believes his wife, Desdemona, is unfaithful, kills her, and kills himself.

Act 1 Iago, a scheming officer wants to take General Otello's place. Iago gets his rival officer, Cassio, drunk so his rank is reduced.

Act 2 To further Cassio's problems, Iago tells Cassio to meet with Otello's wife, Desdemona...and have her ask Otello to restore Cassio's rank. Otello, seeing his wife with Cassio, suspects Cassio is her lover.

Act 3 Iago "creates" further evidence Otello's wife has been unfaithful...a missing handkerchief.

Act 4 Otello strangles Desdemona and then, discovering she was faithful, stabs himself.

PAGLIACCI

Leoncavallo

Actor, Canio stabs his unfaithful actress-wife, Nedda, and her lover, Silvio, in a play within the opera.

Prologue In front of curtain, Tonio, the clown, explains actors have feelings like the rest of us.

Act 1 Actors arrive in town. Tonio, a hunchback clown, makes amorous advances to actress Nedda but is rejected. Nedda arranges to meet local "boyfriend," Silvio, after the performance. Canio, Nedda's husband, overhears. He is angry, but the play must go on.

Act 2 Nedda plays "Columbine." Beppe is "Harlequin," her illicit lover. Canio is "Pagliacci"...who, finding the play too close to real life, stabs his wife, Nedda, and her lover in the audience, Silvio.

PARSIFAL

Wagner

Parsifal recaptures the Spear which pierced Christ. Parsifal then becomes King of the Knights who guard the Holy Grail (cup Jesus used at the Last Supper).

Act 1 Titurel was given the Spear and Holy Cup. Titurel's son, Amfortas, King of Knights which guard the Grail, was wounded by Klingsor, who stole the Spear. The ailing Amfortas conducts a ceremony to consecrate bread and wine.

Act 2 The wicked Klingsor summons a sorceress, Kundry, to his castle. Parsifal defeats them and recaptures the Spear.

Act 3 Parsifal returns the Spear to Knights of Grail, heals Amfortas, and is made King of the Knights.

PORGY AND BESS

Gershwin

A black-culture love story between Porgy, a poor cripple, and Bess, who comes to live with him... and then leaves.

Act 1 Crown kills Robbins at a dice game. Crown flees, and leaves behind his girlfriend, Bess. Bess has no place to live, and Porgy lets her stay with him.

Act 2 Porgy and Bess are happy together. Bess sees Crown at a picnic and is startled. A storm, and the boat of Jake, the fisherman turns over. Crown and Jake's wife, Clara, go to help.

Act 3 Crown returns for Bess, and Porgy kills him. While Porgy is in jail, Sportin' Life, a dope pusher, takes Bess to New York... and Porgy follows them.

I PURITANI
(The Puritans)

Bellini

Love story between Elvira and Lord Arthur.

Act 1 Lord Walter, a Puritan, has engaged his daughter, Elvira, to marry another Puritan, Sir Richard. But, Elvira loves one of the enemy, Lord Arthur...and her father gives in.

Arthur must take Queen Henrietta to safety. Elvira goes crazy, thinking she has been scorned!

Act 2 Elvira is out of her mind; nothing brings back her sanity.

Act 3 Arthur, Elvira's boyfriend, returns...and Elvira regains her sanity! The enemy has been defeated, and Arthur receives a pardon. The lovers, Arthur and Elvira, can now be married!

RHEINGOLD
(Rhinegold)

Wagner

Gold guarded by three Rhine-maidens is stolen. It passes through several hands...until used to pay for Valhalla, a castle for the gods.

Scene 1 An ugly gnome, Alberich, steals gold guarded by the Rhine-maidens.

Scene 2 Wotan, ruler of the gods, and his wife, Fricka, argue about the castle, Valhalla, being built for them by two giants. Fricka's sister, Freia, goddess of youth, is to be exchanged for the castle. The giants say they would accept the Rhinegold instead of Freia...if they receive it by evening.

Scenes 3 & 4 Wotan and Loge, god of fire, trick Alberich and take the gold to pay for the castle.

RIGOLETTO

Verdi

Court jester's daughter falls in love with a Duke...and gives her life to save his.

Act 1 At the Duke's palace, hunchback jester, Rigoletto, entertains the Duke. Monterone curses the Duke for defiling his daughter and is arrested.

Act 2 Duke, disguised as a student, visits jester's daughter, Gilda. Gilda is kidnapped by the Duke's courtiers and taken to the Duke.

Act 3 Rigoletto pleads for his daughter's release...but too late. Her "virtue" has been taken.

Act 4 Rigoletto hires an assassin to kill the Duke. Evening at an inn, Gilda, disguised as a man, manages to be killed instead.

ROMEO AND JULIET

Gounod

Family feud causes tragic love story between Romeo and Juliet.

Act 1 The Capulets hold a masked ball where Romeo (a Montague) meets, and falls in love with, Juliet.

Act 2 Romeo sings to Juliet (a Capulet), who is on her balcony.

Act 3 A secret marriage of Romeo and Juliet by Friar Lawrence. Montagues and Capulets fight; Romeo kills a Capulet. The Duke banishes Romeo from the city.

Act 4 Juliet's father says she must marry Count Paris.

Act 5 Juliet takes a drug that makes her "appear dead." Romeo, thinking Juliet is dead, takes a "real" poison. Juliet awakens as Romeo is dying...and stabs herself.

ROSENKAVALIER
(Cavalier of the Rose)

Richard Strauss

Love story between Octavian and Sophie.

Act 1 Octavian is a young lover of an older, married woman, the Marschallin. The Marschallin suggests Octavian deliver a token of engagement to Sophie...on behalf of her cousin, Baron Ochs.

Act 2 Sophie falls in love with Octavian, the cavalier who delivers the silver rose; Sophie hates the coarse, rude Baron Ochs.

Act 3 Mysterious note invites Baron Ochs to rendezvous at an inn; the Baron is shown to be a scoundrel. Sophie's father, shocked at the baron, now favors Sophie's marriage to Octavian.

SALOME

Richard Strauss

Salome persuades her stepfather, King Herod, to kill John the Baptist, Jokanaan...because Jokanaan rejected Salome's amorous advances.

Act 1 Salome's mother had killed her husband to marry King Herod.

Salome, age 15, seduces Captain of the Guard, Narraboth, to bring John the Baptist, Jokanaan, to her. Captain Narraboth, who loves Salome, kills himself when he discovers Salome prefers Jokanaan.

Jokanaan, rejects Salome's amorous advances...and Salome wants revenge. Salome does "Dance of the Seven Veils" for her stepfather, King Herod...and is granted a wish ...Jokanaan's death and head on a platter! The King grants Salome's wish...and then has her killed.

SAMSON AND DELILAH

Saint-Saens

Delilah takes away Samson's great strength by cutting his hair. With God's help, the blinded captive, Samson, regains his strength...and destroys the pagan temple, killing everyone in it.

Act 1 Samson leads the Israelites in an uprising against their Philistine masters.

Act 2 Delilah seduces Samson and discovers the secret of his great strength. She cuts his hair, weakening him, and he is taken captive and blinded.

Act 3 A child leads the blind Samson into a pagan temple. Samson prays to his God for strength. His prayer answered, Samson is able to destroy the temple...and everyone in it.

LA SERVA PADRONA
(Servant Mistress)

Pergolesi

Comedy about a maid, Serpina, who persuades her bachelor-master, Uberto, to marry her.

Act 1 Bachelor, Uberto, decides his maid Serpina, is too high-spirited and independent to follow his orders. He decides to find a wife, who will put the maid in her place. Uberto tells his mute valet, Vespone, to find him a wife. The maid, Serpina, decides **she** would make the best wife for Uberto.

Act 2 Serpina disguises the mute valet as her suitor, "Captain Tempesta"...who demands a big dowery...or that Uberto, himself, marry Serpina. Uberto decides to marry Serpina.

SIEGFRIED

Wagner

Siegfried (grandson of Wotan, king of the gods) grows into manhood; kills a dragon and captures a magic golden ring and a hat that can make him invisible; and discovers the sleeping Brunnhilde.

Act 1 Siegfried's mother, Sieglinde, died giving birth to him. Thus, Siegfried is raised by a gnome named Mime. Siegfried forges a magic sword from broken pieces of his father Siegmund's sword.

Act 2 Siegfried kills a powerful dragon with his sword...and takes the magic ring and magic hat the dragon was guarding.

Act 3 Siegfried finds, and awakens, Brunnhilde, once a warrior-goddess, who is now a mortal.

LA SONNAMBULA
(The Sleepwalker)

Bellini

A sleepwalking girl, Amina, is thought to be unfaithful to her fiance, Elvino...because she is found in a strange man's bed! Later, people see her walking in her sleep. Now her jealous boyfriend, Elvino, understands... and loves her again.

Act 1 An engagement party celebrates Amina's betrothal to Elvino. That night, sleepwalking, Amina enters the room of a stranger at the inn, Count Rodolfo. Startled, the Count leaves the room. Amina is later discovered in his bed!

Act 2 Amina's angry boyfriend, Elvino, takes his engagement ring from her finger. Then the villagers see Amina sleepwalking...and Elvino realizes Amina is innocent!

TALES OF HOFFMANN
(Contes d'Hoffmann)

Offenbach

In a tavern, Hoffmann tells his romances with Olympia, a mechanical doll; Giulietta, a courtesan; and Antonia, a singer.

Prologue At a tavern with friend Nicklausse, Hoffmann tells of the women he loved and lost.

Act 1 Olympia, a beautiful mechanical doll, looks real through magic glasses given Hoffmann.

Act 2 Giulietta steals Hoffmann's soul (reflection in a mirror)...then runs off with Pittichinaccio.

Act 3 Hoffmann loves Antonia, a singer, who is killed by Dr. Miracle.

Epilogue Stella, the actress, sees Hoffmann drunk in the tavern...and leaves with Lindorf.

TANNHAUSER

Wagner

Tannhauser battles with the dilemma of love with one woman...or love with many women.

Act 1 Tannhauser is with Venus, goddess of love, and her nymphs, experiencing illicit love. He calls upon the Virgin Mary...and Venus' evil court disappears.

Tannhauser goes to Landgrave, whose daughter Elisabeth loves Tannhauser with a pure love.

Act 2 At a singing contest Tannhauser sings the joys of illicit love, shocking everyone. The Landgrave orders Tannhauser to Rome for a pardon from the Pope.

Act 3 Elisabeth dies waiting for Tannhauser. The Pope refuses a pardon until his Holy Staff sprouts leaves...which happens!

THAIS

Massenet

A monk, Athanael, converts Thais, beautiful woman of pleasure, to Christianity. As Thais is dying, Athanael realizes he loves her.

Act 1 In the desert with other monks, Athanael decides to return to Alexandria, Egypt, to save Thais' soul. In Alexandria, his rich friend, Nicias, provides Athanael with fresh clothes.

Act 2 Athanael persuades Thais to leave her life of erotic luxury and come with him. She leaves all her possessions...and burns down her house.

Act 3 At a desert oasis, Athanael gives Thais to Abbess Albine for a convent. Later he realizes he loves Thais. Athanael arrives at the convent as Thais is dying.

TOSCA

Puccini

Tragic death of a singer, Tosca, and the painter, Cavaradossi, she loved.

Act 1 Angelotti, an escaped political prisoner, hurries into Church. Cavaradossi, who is painting a mural, finds Angelotti... and hides him. Tosca, Cavaradossi's girlfriend comes to Church.

Act 2 Cavaradossi is tortured by police for helping Angelotti escape. Tosca promises herself to Scarpia, Rome's chief of police, to free Cavaradossi. After Scarpia gives her two safe conduct passes to leave the city...Tosca stabs him.

Act 3 Cavaradossi must face a "fake" execution. Instead, bullets are real! Cavaradossi is killed... and Tosca jumps to her death.

LA TRAVIATA
(The Strayed One)

Verdi

Alfredo falls in love with Violetta, "lady of pleasure" to French high society. Alfredo's father, Giorgio, disapproves...and tells Violetta this affair will prevent Alfredo's sister from marrying. So, Violetta rejects Alfredo even though she loves him!

Act 1 Alfredo meets Violetta at a party, and they fall in love.

Act 2 Alfredo and Violetta live in a country cottage. Violetta sells her jewelry to pay bills. Alfredo's father asks Violetta to end the affair; she returns to Paris.

Not understanding Violetta's motives, Alfredo insults her and her escort, Baron Douphol, at a party.

Act 3 Alfredo returns to Violetta ...as she is dying.

TRISTAN UND ISOLDE

Wagner

Love story between Tristan and Isolde...whom Tristan must take to marry his Uncle, King Marke.

Act 1 Isolde is a sorceress-princess. Tristan killed her boy-friend, Morold. Wounded in the fight, Tristan is nursed back to health by Isolde.

Isolde is angry because Tristan is taking her to marry his Uncle, King Marke. Isolde's attendant, Brangaene, gives Tristan and Isolde a love potion.

Act 2 At King Marke's palace, Tristan and Isolde meet...are discovered...and Tristan is wounded.

Act 3 Tristan is dying at his castle. Isolde comes to Tristan, and they die together.

IL TROVATORE
(The Troubadour)

Verdi

Tragic love between singing knight, Manrico, and lady, Leonora.

Act 1 Leonora loves a mysterious knight who serenades her. Knight, Manrico, returns...and fights young Count di Luna.

Act 2 Azucena tells other gypsies how she kidnapped one of old Count's two sons...and raised him as her own son, Manrico. Manrico rescues Leonora from a convent.

Act 3 Azucena, Manrico's gypsy-foster mother, is captured...and Manrico is taken trying to free her.

Act 4 Leonora offers herself to free Manrico. The young Count agrees; then Leonora takes poison. The young Count kills Manrico... then discovers he killed his brother!

TURANDOT

Puccini

The "Unknown Prince," Calaf, answers Chinese Princess Turandot's three riddles...and marries her.

Act 1 The Prince of Persia is killed because he failed to answer Princess Turandot's three riddles. In the crowd is Timur, former king of tartars...with his servant-girl, Liu, and his son, Calaf.

Act 2 "Unknown Prince," Calaf, answers all three riddles. Turandot is unhappy, so he tells her she may avoid marriage, and even kill him, if she learns his name by morning.

Act 3 Liu is tortured but refuses to reveal the "Unknown Prince's" name. Liu loves him and stabs herself to avoid telling. Turandot softens...falls in love with Calaf.

DIE WALKURE
(The Valkyrie)

Wagner

Wotan, ruler of the gods, and Erda, the earth Goddess had nine warrior-daughters (Valkyries). Valkyrie Brunnhilde disobeys Wotan ...and he condemns her to become a mortal, go into deep sleep, and marry the first man who finds her.

Act 1 Siegmund finds Sieglinde, his sister, married to Hunding. The brother and sister flee together, taking a magic sword with them.

Act 2 Wotan commands Brunnhilde not to aid them, but she saves the pregnant Sieglinde.

Act 3 For disobeying him, Wotan puts Brunnhilde to sleep...and surrounds her with a circle of fire so that only a "brave" man will come through the fire to find her.

Autographs:

Autographs:

Autographs:

Autographs:

Autographs:

Autographs:

Autographs:

Autographs: